Quilters are a special breed. Always generous, you teach each other, inspire one another, and share ideas, chocolate, and stories. My goodness the stories! The things we have heard from you as you've visited us or written to us have changed the way we see the world, and we never cease to be amazed by your incredible stories of generosity, heritage, and resilience.

Ever since our story contest for National Quilting Month in March 2014, which we repeated in 2015, we have opened our mailbox and our hearts to your stories and we have been richly rewarded. Every week we receive more stories of the experiences that have brought you to quilting, some heartbreaking, some heartwarming, and a few that make us laugh out loud.

Collecting these stories has become a particularly special part of what we do here. As we read about the reasons you quilt and we laugh or cry along with you, we realize more than ever that we are part of a worldwide quilting family.

Thanks for sharing your stories and for being part of our family.

Jenny

P.S. If you have a story to share, send it on over to stories@missouriquiltco.com, and watch for more stories every Tuesday at missouriquiltco.com/shop/dailydeal.

The Quilter's Support Network

by **LEO DUMONT**
San Martin, California

I am not a quilter, but I play an active role in the life of the quilter who agreed to make me her spouse.

I have been in every quilt shop from California to Minnesota, except those that were closed.

My job at the Quilter's Support Network is complex; I am required to stop at every quilt store in every town, wait patiently, and be ready to voice my opinion between two identical-looking blue fabrics.

I am also obligated to pull out my wallet and pay for these purchases, which I don't mind, because fabric doesn't spoil and it makes her happy. Some years back I had to fork over for a new sewing machine and that was a bit more painful.

As a full time employee, I'm mandated to attend the Pacific International Quilt Show, as both driver and sherpa. I'm also supposed to keep my

Photo Courtesy Leo Dumont

eyes in my head while being in a room with 10,000 beautiful women who know how to sew.

My most critical mission, however, is to play "One of these things is not like the other; one of these things does not belong." I knew all those years of watching Sesame Street would pay off, and I'm pretty good at picking out the quilt block my spouse is unhappy with.

Finally, I have to tell you how working for this Support Network has paid off. My day job sent me to a conference. It was in a very small town that had a bar, a restaurant, and a quilt shop. The conference started at nine a.m. At seven I had already eaten breakfast, and at eight, the bar was just out of the question. I walked into the quilt shop, and those wonderful, beautiful, quilting women all came to help me. Over the next hour they showed me quilts and fat quarters and even sold me a ticket for a quilt raffle.

And guess what? I won.

My wife and all her quilting buddies are still green with envy.

So Many Reasons to Quilt

by **LINDA COOK DEVONA**
Afton, New York

I quilt for many, many reasons. It's a wonderful way to introduce more color into my life, especially during our long, drab winters. I can't resist ordering the tempting charm packs from MSQC, even ones that are outside the comfort zone of my favorite colors (blues and greens). I like traditional designs, but depending on my mood or something in the air, I might even order something wild and quirky. It's fun to live a little dangerously now and then!

I quilt to connect to women in my past who quilted because they needed to keep their families warm. I treasure a Sunbonnet Sue quilt my grandma made for my mom when she was little out of scraps from her homemade 1920s dresses. My mom continued the tradition and made me a Sunbonnet Sue quilt out of some of my girlhood dresses; there's even a block made with scraps from my sixth grade graduation dress in 1966.

Photo Courtesy Linda Cook Devona

Quilting connects me to the future as well as the past. Everyone I know and care about who gets married or has a baby gets a homemade quilt. As long as people get married, have birthdays, or have babies, there is always a reason to make quilts to honor them. Quilters always have something to create, so we're never bored! Yesterday, my niece, Sara, called to tell us she's expecting a baby in September! ! Another reason to play with my stash!

Quilting helps me to work through my loss of loved ones. I made a floral quilt for my mom's bed when she had to go to the nursing home in 2010. It was a small way to help me deal with the transition and to cloak her

Photo Courtesy Linda Cook Devona

with my love as well. After my beloved dad died in 2011, I couldn't bear to dispose of his closet full of church shirts, consisting of mostly pale, striped pastels. I've made a small quilt for one of his granddaughters, and with the leftovers I may piece curtain panels for my sewing room. He would be glad, I'm sure, since he grew up during the depression, and knew how to make use of every small scrap of wire, twist tie, and plastic bag.

I love to quilt because it's part of who I am. I may not be a quilter's quilter with precisely pieced points, but I'm a loving quilter who loves the endless possibilities of creating special quilts to honor those I love!

Alicia,
quilting and the
military life have a lot
in common. People come and
go in your military career, but the
friendships endure.
Projects half-done (PhD)
move in and out, with
memories enduring, t
Peggy
P.S. Post pics of yo
beautiful daugh

Feathering the Empty Nest

by **TABBY BUDDE**
Cape Coral, Florida

I'm so excited to share my story because without Missouri Star Quilt Co, I may never have learned to quilt. I am a forty-five year-old mother of one lovely daughter. Approximately three years ago my daughter met her now-husband and dumped me! Well that's how it felt anyway, but actually she just left the nest as children are supposed to do.

I remember thinking, "Oh Lord, what am I going to do now? My best friend just left me... here... alone... with my husband!" My husband, being the wise and caring man he is, thought if I picked up something to do as a hobby it may help mend my broken heart and put a smile on my face, because as everyone knows, "When the queen is happy there is peace in the kingdom!"

Photo Courtesy Tabby Budde

I was shopping one evening at our local craft shop and happened upon the sewing section. Now, I have never sewed a day in my life but I was drawn to the beautiful quilts and embroidered designs that were displayed. I went home and mentioned to my husband that maybe I'd pick up sewing but I really don't know how and I"m busy at work and blah blah blah. Well, the light bulb went on in his head and next thing I knew he bought me a Singer Futura machine that does machine embroidery and quilting! Holy cow! Now I HAD to learn to sew.

But what to do? Where to go? Ahhh! The University of Youtube to the rescue! I found Jenny on Youtube and binge-watched her videos, with each video building in me the courage to give quilting a go. I'm happy to report I have made many quilts since then as gifts and for myself. My most current love is making tote bags, which I learned from Jenny as well with the jelly roll tote bag tutorial.

I'm happy to report I have survived my "empty nest" syndrome and have even discovered how much I love being with my husband again. He is also a wonderful quilting helper; he does any quilting math I may need and is a wonderful fabric cutter!

Not the Right Shade of Maroon

by **D.Q. TODISCO**
North Andover, Massachusetts

Many years ago (more than I care to remember) my big sister graduated from college, met the man of her dreams, and finally moved back home to New England. How excited I was to have my big sister back! She came back home with a new hobby... quilting.

Wanting to spend all our free time together, I let her drag me from quilt shop to quilt shop and oh, how I dreaded those day-long quilt shows she would take me to. But I loved being with her, and going to lunch afterwards was guaranteed laughter and fun. At one quilt show we attended, she kept asking my opinion of this particular line of fabric. I smiled and said it was lovely as I looked down at my watch hoping we still had time to have a late lunch somewhere.

Some years later, I was busy decorating our new home and my sister presented me with a quilt. I remember how excited she was to show it to me, as it was almost complete. She proudly held up the quilt and flung it up into the air so that it gracefully fell upon the floor showing a beautiful array of burnt red colored fabrics. Unbeknownst to me, these were the fabrics that I liked at that quilt show so long ago. "It's the wrong shade of maroon," I told her, thinking of my home's color-scheme, and that was all I said. I forgot about the quilt and life went on.

Many, many years later, my son was filling out college applications and how my heart broke to see him leave the nest. What could I send him off to college with that would be a reminder of my love? A quilt made by his mom would be the perfect gift, I thought. My sister was thrilled beyond words. She gave me an old sewing machine she wasn't using anymore. She gave me a quilting hoop, so I could hand stitch the top of the quilt. But when she offered me her rotary cutter and quilting supplies, I told her I didn't need any of those useless gadgets. I had a twelve-inch straight ruler and my kitchen scissors could do the job. Then, to my sister's dismay, I purchased my fabric at a local craft store. I paid no attention to her words of wisdom regarding the difference between local craft shop fabrics and quality quilting fabrics, like the kind sold at Missouri Star Quilt Co.

And so my first quilt began by cutting five-inch squares out of a few yards of fabric. My hands were hurting from the scissors and some of my squares were not even, but I was determined to finish the quilt before my son left for school. I stayed up late at night sewing each block together. My sister smiled at the collection of blocks I managed to sew together, and she helped me with the muslin backing and taught me how to hand stitch the top of the quilt using quilting tape and a thimble.

So my son went off to college with that quilt, my special gift of love to him. The last time I saw the quilt, it was hanging on the rocking chair next to my tiny granddaughter's crib. What sweet tears I shed as I picked up that tattered and worn quilt. The binding I had hand-stitched was all but gone, some of the prints had worn off my craft store fabric, and a lot of the seams had opened up. My mind went back to my sister telling me to machine stitch the binding, and how important it was to make quarter-inch seams. But wow, the quilt sure did look like it was loved! I wrapped that quilt around my shoulders and my eyes flooded with tears. Even years after his college graduation, that old tattered quilt still remained in his possession. Yes, my quilt was all about the love I have for him.

Well, I eventually learned my lesson about quality fabric after that first quilt, how to properly cut fabric with the necessary tools, and the reason for a quarter-inch seam allowance. With the start and completion of each quilt I have made for my family over the many years, my mind always travels back to that first quilt. No, not the one I made for my son, but rather the one that got away. The one I call "Not the Right Shade of Maroon".

For those of us who are blessed to have a sister, we value not only their love and friendship, but their knowledge as well. They lead the way for us in so many ways throughout our lives, and sometimes they teach us without even knowing. "Not the Right Shade of Maroon" is my favorite story about quilting because it taught me that a quilt is more than just a blanket. It's a symbol of love. "Not the Right Shade of Maroon" is still on the chair in my sister's family room and each time I see it, I am reminded of her love.

If you are wondering why I never apologized, believe me I did! But there are lessons to learn as we go through life, and learning to be grateful for the people in your life is one of them. So I thank my sister for teaching me the art of quilting, and more important I thank her for teaching me gratitude.

Quilting Like a Boss

by **LEANNE HINES HILL**
Cape Coral, Florida

Once upon a time, long, long ago, in a land far, far away, I was assistant treasurer of a family-owned oil/petroleum transportation and storage company. My boss, the chief financial officer, decided to do some team-building to get all of his direct-reports to communicate with him more. He hired a couple of psychologists that did that sort of thing and got us a conference room at a downtown hotel for the requisite number of days to spend team building. The psychologists sent us a bunch of personality and IQ tests to take beforehand, the results of which they would share with us at the conference.

I have an MBA in Accounting and Finance and this job entailed running the treasury operations of the company. I made sure wire payments were made on time and accurately, negotiated letters of credit guaranteeing payment on cargoes of petroleum products to our trading partners, and worked 12-hour days pretty regularly. But on weekends, I would quilt, having learned the art three or four years earlier.

One weekend I went into my favorite quilt store and bought a pattern and all the fabric to complete a Kansas Trouble wall hanging which I then finished that weekend; we were negotiating a loan agreement that had gone on for a few months and I had to FINISH something. But I digress...

The team-building conference began and all of the CFO's direct-reports trooped into the downtown hotel's conference room. One of the psychologists asked a group of us women which one I was. They asked me what I did that was creative because I had tested "off the charts in creativity." I told them I make quilts!

They told me that was good and to keep it up. I do!

Knight in Shining Thimble

by **EILEEN DYETT**
Cortland, Ohio

Once upon a time I used to complain that I hated having to pack up all my sewing equipment when I had to use the dining room table to serve a meal to my family. Why couldn't we just eat off TV trays? But we had no extra rooms and no funds to add on to the house.

Then one day I came home after work to discover that my husband had used his day off to put up a wall across part of our large L-shaped living room. He was pleased with himself, and I offered to write to the Vatican and put forth his case for sainthood! Soon I had a small sewing room complete with a pegboard wall for hanging notions, a spool rack for thread, a pocket door for privacy, a fold-up wall-mounted cutting table, and he even built me a solid oak sewing cabinet. See what I mean about sainthood?

Flash forward ten years and I have moved from sewing clothing and curtains into quilting which requires sooo much more fabric and supplies. I found that my perfect little sewing getaway is cramped and much too small.

Again, I arrived home one day to find that Hubby has moved my sewing cabinet into our family room and installed built-in shelving and counters! He said that since our sons were grown and we didn't need a gathering room for teenagers any longer, I should have a bigger space. I now have room for a short arm quilting machine and frame, and I LOVE the spaciousness.

By the way, my former sewing room now houses my stash. And my dear husband and I are living happily ever after.

The end.

Pride Goes Before a Fall

by **GINNY GALVIN**
Jonesboro, Georgia

I was traveling from Boston to California to visit my brother and attend his wedding. Knowing the hours I would spend on the plane, I decided I would bring the lap quilt I was working on and do the finishing hand stitching and quilting. I sat in my window seat with my quilt spread all over my lap, sewing away and feeling so self righteous. I was not wasting my time snoozing or looking at out-dated magazines. I would have something to show for my five hours of sitting.

Finally the attendant announced that we would be landing in ten minutes and it was time to prepare for landing. I waited to finish a last line of stitching and put all my needles and threads and other supplies in their baggie. I planned to fold the quilt back into its carry-on when we touched down and then I could stand up.

As I started to fold the quilt I realized that I had stitched it onto my wool slacks in two places. There was NO WAY I could get it undone before we had to get off. You can imagine the questioning stares as I walked out into the airport with a bright colored quilt hanging off me. When my brother looked questioningly at me as I came out of the restricted area I smiled, and said "Don't ask." The pride was gone from the beginning of the flight and I now was in the fall period. Each time I look at this quilt it reminds me that you can't win them all!

Piecing Together Peace of Mind

by **JESSICA MARCILLO**
Fort Sill, Oklahoma

When did quilting change my life forever? Well, I started quilting in 2010 during my husband's second tour in Iraq. During his first tour I spent time back home with my mom who taught me my way around a sewing machine. That is also when I learned how to make pajama pants and now I can practically make them in my sleep, I tell ya!

Once the second tour came about my kiddo was in the first grade and I had a full day of wondering what else I could do to keep my mind occupied and off of the things that worried me most. I could have very easily gotten together with other wives but I am not necessarily a social butterfly and besides, I felt it was easier not to get involved in any sort of group who may only talk about all the horrific things that could go wrong. (Being a veteran myself my imagination doesn't need to stretch far for those possibilities.) In my mind it was simpler to keep my social

Photo Courtesy Jessica Marcillo

circle small to include my little guy, my superman that the army had way too far away, and my dear family back home.

In the spring of 2010 I was kind of burnt out on making pajama pants, which is about the time I discovered the awesomeness of tutorials on YouTube and the even greater awesomeness of Jenny Doan! Now, I am not trying to earn any brownie points from anyone there at MSQC by saying this, but it is a known fact that Jenny Doan and the entire Doan family can be found in an encyclopedia under people and things that are awesome! Just stating a simple fact. When I saw my first tutorial done by Jenny I was hooked right away!

My favorite project during that time was one I made towards the end of deployment on Thanksgiving Day. My son and I enjoyed the day and I made a small turkey for just the two of us. I fit in sewing breaks between playing with my son, checking the turkey, and shooing the cats off the sewing table! Once the turkey was put away, the cats had their fill, and the kiddo was in bed, I was able to sit back down and complete my table runner. That moment is precisely when I officially caught the quilting bug! It's also when I fully realized how quilting was able to give me peace of mind and joy even during what was one of the most difficult times in my life. To this day I consider it a form of therapy and an act of love that I can also use to give to the ones I love and those in need!

The Healing Power of Quilting

by **MELINA GRANTHAM STANTON**
Silsbee, Texas

My stepmother Geraldine had a catastrophic car accident in January of this year, and between surgeries to repair broken bones, rehab, an awful gall bladder removal, more rehab, and several stints in a nursing home and the ER for various complications, she finally came home for the first time in April.

She had quilted and sewn years before and loved it; however with a very demanding full-time job, she hadn't done any in many years. But she continued to she collect fabric for years, confident that when she retired, she would return to quilting.

Well now she was forced into retirement, having literally months of doctor visits and therapy ahead of her. She began going through her stash and quilting as part of her occupational therapy.

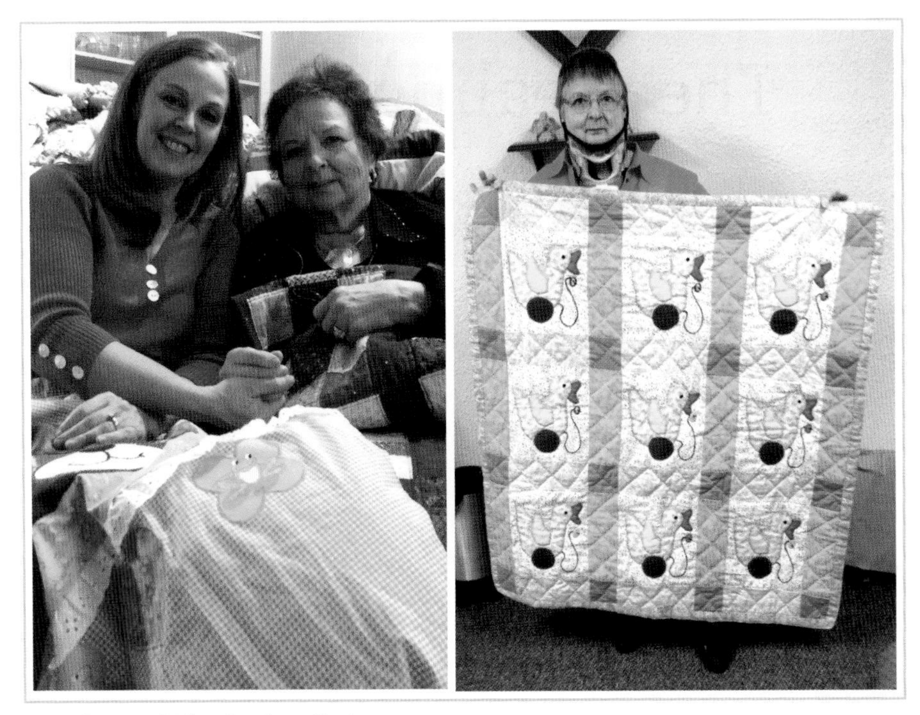

Photo Courtesy Melina Grantham Stanton

She made this beautiful baby quilt, appliquéd by hand, without a recipient in mind, waiting for God to show her someone. One day at a doctor's appointment her nurse told her about her neighbor who had recently had a baby, a year after losing a baby and being told she would never carry one to term. This baby was truly a miracle! Immediately Geraldine knew this baby needed this quilt, for it symbolized the miracle in her own life: that she survived at all, that she walked and talked again, and that she could even have such fine motor control to be able to hand sew!

Needless to say, the mother was overwhelmed by the gift. Since that first quilt she has been cranking new ones out at an impressive rate, and finishing ones she started up to fifty years ago!

Another huge benefit of quilting is how close we have become since her accident. Throughout her hospitalization and recovery we have spent more time together than ever, and afterward we became quilting buddies. I taught her how to machine piece and quilt and we joined our local guild. We look forward to many quilts together!

Quilting Comfort

by **KAY VON DER EMBSE**
Springboro, Ohio

My husband's great grandfather migrated to the U.S. from Germany in the 1800s. There had been little connection between that German family and the U.S. family until my stepson happened to find a family member, Torsten, in Hanover, Germany, through the internet. One great use for the internet! Through a series of events, we met Torsten's aunt when she brought her students to visit the Indianapolis 500 Museum. We quickly became family and visited them in Germany shortly thereafter. They welcomed us into their home as if we had known each other forever and a family tie was established. A while later we learned that the aunt had developed Stage 4 breast cancer.

My first thought was, "Oh my goodness, she needs a quilt!" I'm in Ohio, and I called my quilting buddy who lives in Indiana to ask her what she was doing over the coming weekend. I told her about wanting to make a quilt in a hurry to send to Germany and she made plans to come right over. We cut and sewed and pieced and pieced and sewed, only taking breaks for meals and a quick run to the quilt shop for the right color fabric. We decided on a log cabin pattern since it would go a little faster and made it in peach and cream colors. Over the next week we quilted and put the binding on and shipped it off to Germany.

I received a thank you note from Torsten's aunt asking how we knew exactly what colors her bedroom was done in. I will never know why we chose those particular colors but it gave her comfort. Our comfort came in knowing that we had provided a message of hope and love in a tangible form since we could not be there to hug her ourselves.

Quilting is a Gift

by **BARBARA BUTLER**
Denton, Texas

I had only been quilting for one year, and my first project was a king size quilt with sashing & posts. It's far from perfect, but it looks great on our bed. My teacher said, "If you can't see the mistake riding by on horseback, then no one will notice!" Texas women have great sayings!

That was the year I caught quilt fever. I turned a spare bedroom into my quilting room, but put the computer in there to justify it. It's also the "office." I needed to be able to watch MSQC tutorials! My husband never said a word, smart man!

I was itching to start another quilt, and a friend suggested I make a lap quilt for my dad who was in a nursing home at eighty years old. I went to the quilt store and asked for help, where a wonderful woman helped me pick a simple pattern and the fat quarters I'd need. She told me to read through the instructions first then go back to the beginning to start

Photo Courtesy Barbara Butler

I'm the one with my hair up! The other woman is Beth Waddell, my best friend who lives in Kansas City, Mo.

cutting. I finished it and was able to send it to Dad in Ohio only four days late for his birthday, Christmas Eve.

I was in Pittsburgh for New Years with a friend, when my sister called to tell me my dad was in the hospital in critical care. My sweet friend drove me to Cleveland at eleven at night and we prayed all night at his bedside. He woke up and over the next two days we laughed and told stories as his health improved.

When I asked about his present he said he never opened it because he felt too bad to get up. My lovely little sister went to his room at the nursing home and retrieved the box. I got to see my Dad open his quilt! He was so surprised and said, "You made this for me?"

I knew how special giving someone a quilt is because it made him so happy. He just beamed and mentioned it to every nurse and doctor that came in the room! It was such a gift to get to experience all this instead of just a phone call.

Unfortunately, his health declined and he passed a week later in his own bed, under his new quilt. I donated the quilt to hospice because they had been so good to him. I've given away three more quilts since then and it is such a joy to make them! Now I talk to the quilts as I make them, wishing the recipients good lives and many blessings. Quilting has opened a new space in my life for giving love.

Carrying on the Tradition

by **KATHI HUEBNER**
Amana, Iowa

My Aunt Darleen, everyone's favorite aunt in the family, never married and lived with our grandparents. She took us to the circus, Ice-capades, went on vacations with us all over the U.S., came to our concerts, and when we had children, she gave us baby books to keep our memories as they grew.

One year, she learned to make "quillows" and asked each of us to choose a theme for one to decorate our homes. She gave them to us for our birthdays, and we used them until they were threadbare. They can be used as pillows or quilts, and on particularly cold nights we would stick our feet into the pillow pocket to keep extra warm. My sisters and I folded them every night back into neat pillows. We LOVED those quillows!

When my middle son was born, I asked her to make him a quillow for Christmas. It was an adorable quillow and as he grew he loved to

Photo Courtesy Kathi Huebner

snuggle in it when he watched TV with me at night. Ethan was born in August and she made that quillow in the fall. She passed away a month after Christmas. It was the last gift she made.

A few years back, as I was going through chemo for breast cancer, my sister asked me to make an Iowa State Cyclones quillow for my brother-in-law for Christmas. I was bored to tears at home, and it helped me to focus on something else. I actually got it made in time, and he loves it! My sister even folds it up every night into a neat pillow. For a wedding gift, I made a pieced quilt for my nephew and his new wife, and turned

Photos Courtesy Kathi Huebner

it into a quillow. The pattern was X's and O's. I posted a picture of it on Facebook and my cousins started commenting, "Is that like the ones Aunt Darleen made us?" I didn't know she had made them for all of her nieces and nephews, but the memories came rushing out from all over the U.S. We all have the original ones she made.

Once I had made the one for my nephew, I decided to make them for the amazing women who work with me for their birthdays. It has taken longer than I anticipated, but each one reflects something about each woman. The master gardener who is in charge of the Butterfly Exhibit at the fair was the first one to receive her quillow. It has butterflies, flowers, and dragonflies, and the pillow flap is quilted with a dragonfly stencil and gorgeous thread.

The Detroit Red Wings are next in a zipper pattern, a disappearing nine patch with gorgeous floral prints is ready for the backing, and the batik one with the Disappearing Pinwheel #3 pattern is going together smoothly. My niece will get a pinwheel one with Ashford charm packs and batiks, my sister is in line for one made from Concerto fabric, my other niece was proposed to by her husband at the top of the Eiffel Tower, so hers will be Paris fabric. My son will get flannels/plaids, my daughter-in-law wants one from the Lorax line, another son wants woodland creatures, and my granddaughter is set with Simply Gorjuss. My other sister has brown/beige batiks picked out. The MSQC tutorials have been awesome in helping me find just the right look for each quilt.

Is that a lot to do? Yes. Is it worth it to carry on the tradition that this incredible woman started? Yes. People should experience being wrapped up in the love of family and friends. I hope they use them until they're threadbare.

The Gift That Keeps on Giving

by **PATTY C. SAUL**
Crozet, Virginia

My cousin is from the Hershey/Lancaster area of Pennsylvania and has quilted beautifully forever. About nine years ago, she came to my house and said she was going to teach me how to make my three sons a quilt for Christmas. After my sister and mother picked themselves off the floor from laughing, she told me the plan. You see, I was the one left out of the talent department. My sister and mother were the go-to people if you wanted something made or crafted. I didn't even know where the bobbin was in the sewing machine!

Elaine brought all the equipment: sewing machine, mat, rotary cutter, thread, etc. and taught me how to make a simple block quilt for each of them. She stood beside me as I learned to cut and measure, chain sew, put on borders, and finally, stitch in the ditch. When she wasn't around, I had to get a friend to show me how to put thread on the bobbin! She even showed me how to copy pictures on fabric and look for special blocks for each of the boys that showed their specific interests. Well, I was hooked! The adventure of looking for special material and colors fascinated me.

I was determined to NOT to buy too much material for the project so as to avoid leftovers and NOT to buy material that I had no pattern for. Hah! The next time Elaine came down, I had one extra tote full, then three totes full, then... I refuse to tell you how many totes and drawers there are now!

Quilting is my therapy, my relief from stress, and my place to go when I want to create something beautiful for someone else. I pray over the quilts I make for others and feel like I am giving a part of myself to them. Elaine gave quite a gift to me that fall. I am eternally grateful and so very blessed.

She Never Made One For Herself

by **ROBIN OQUIST**
Eagle Point, Oregon

My friend Peggy loved Jenny and loved quilting. She got me started watching MSQC tutorials. Every night at ten p.m. (midnight MSQC time) she had to see what the new deal was before it sold out. I think she ordered every week.

She made seven or eight quilts in the last two years and every table runner and purse that Jenny has done. She learned to quilt from watching Jenny.

Peggy died Thanksgiving weekend age fifty-nine. Mini stroke. Her last quilt was the curvy log cabin. Peggy never made a quilt for herself; she made them for friends, neighbors, cousins, but not one for herself. So her husband said the curvy log cabin isn't going anywhere.

Photo Courtesy Robin Oquist

I just got the quilt back from my quilter, Carol, who, by the way, quilted it out of the goodness of her heart. The quilt is so rich, all in batiks. Carol quilted it with leaves and she used a turquoise thread. It's so beautiful on the batik black border. Bernie is going to love this quilt so much. I just hope he uses a tissue when he receives it at Christmas, I don't want that quilt messed up!

During the Twilight Hours

by **MICHELE RUTOLO**
Sinking Spring, Pennsylvania

You never know how much a quilt impacts the recipient until you see it with your own eyes. I was lucky enough to have that experience with my dad. He was afflicted with Lewey Body Disease which affects the brain, one of the results being dementia. When my dad became bedridden, I took early retirement to help my mom care for him at their home and would go there every day to help. For some reason I became his 'trigger' back to reality and the hospice nurses would call me during particularly bad mornings asking me to come earlier than normal. My dad would snap out of his downward spiral within minutes of my arrival.

Prior to this point I had signed up to attend a three-day quilt retreat with my guild an hour from home. My dad became agitated when he heard I was going away; both parents relied on my daily visits. To comfort him,

Photo Courtesy Michele Rutolo

my mom (a non-quilter) told him I would make him a quilt while I was at the retreat and give it to him for his birthday... just a week and a half away! His smile grew and he calmed, but the pressure was on!

I don't usually buy kits, but one had called out to me during a quilt show and I bought it on the spot. It was perfect for my dad, an avid hiker and outdoors-man all his life who was raised on a small farm. It was a nine-patch with every other block a patch of toile scenes of children playing in the woods, including a barn and even a dog (he loved my dogs, especially my black lab). The outer border of pine trees growing on a mountain would be nostalgic as well.

Could I cut and piece it all in time? My friends had all been pulling for me, offering encouragement and telling me I could do it. I worked feverishly from 6:00 a.m. until midnight and finished it within fifteen minutes of packing up at the end of the retreat. Now how was I to quilt it while being at my parents home the better part of every day? I knew I couldn't finish it in a week.

Did I mention that people who quilt are special? I find them to be kind, generous, giving people with huge hearts. My friend Janice, a professional long-arm quilter with deadlines of her own, stepped up and moved it ahead of her existing jobs to quilt it for me. I was hand stitching the binding an hour before his birthday party.

We were all reduced to tears when my dad saw it. The smile on his face was priceless! It was the best birthday gift I ever gave him, as well as the last. He slept under that quilt every day from November until he passed away in August. He would get agitated at night even in the warm weather if he didn't have it; simply feeling it would calm him down.

That quilt was made under pressure, but I was surrounded with encouragement and help from my friends who knew how important it was to me, and it was made with love. Who knew a quilt could mean so much? By the way, the label I made read: "Given with love to my dad to keep him warm during his twilight hours." It did that and SO much more!

Nothing to Do But Quilt

by **LINDA LEE STOVALL**
Florence, Oregon

The year was 1970. The place was San Diego, California. Growing up as a city girl, I was used to a lot of external excitement and didn't have any experience in spending quiet hours entertaining myself.

I was twenty-three years old and had been married a year. We had just become parents for the first time. I had never met my husband's relatives in person because they lived too far away for them to be able to travel to us. It seemed natural that my husband would want to introduce me and his new son to them, so we packed up our little compact car and started off for West Virginia. After a day of rest at his parents' home, we were taken here and there to visit grandparents, lots of cousins, uncles, and aunts.

We stayed two nights with my husband's grandmother who lived very near the Ohio River. There was no television there and no radio. Talk about culture shock! There was a large porch on the front of the house and a large hanging swing. She and I were sitting and swinging one

Photo Courtesy Linda Lee Stovall

evening. The air was thick and warm with the twinkle of lightning bugs here and there. It was very quiet. She seemed to be having a good time just sitting and swinging.

The next afternoon it was back to the swing and more quietness. I shyly asked her: “Is there anything that people do here other than watch the grass grow?” Asking me to wait, she got up, went into the house, and brought out a shoebox that was full of tiny squares of fabric. I did not have a clue what they were for. She gave me a needle and thread and she threaded up. Then she showed me how to sew them together. When we left she sent some squares and a cardboard template along with me.

When we returned home I experimented cutting out squares with the little template until I my fingers blistered. I did not have much of an attention span then and could not imagine sewing by hand, thousands of postage sized squares together to make something the size of a quilt. I gave up on that project and experimented with larger size patches. I did not know that I should buy 100% cotton. I thought I was supposed to cut things up from around the house, which is what I did. I cut up old polyester, double knit, cotton, and who knows what. After a very long time I had my first quilt top. Many of the seams did not match and where I used double knit there were volcano intersections. I found an old sheet and used it as a backing. I could not quilt it by hand or any other way.

I learned several things from that first experience, and for some crazy reason I wanted to try again. I started hoarding little bits of fabric from here and there, putting it into boxes according to colors and I started buying fabric to use as backgrounds and backings.

My son is now forty-three years old and I am still sewing, quilting and learning. I have my completed quilts stuffed into every chest, on every bed, on the walls, on almost every shelf and any spot I can find. I love and treasure my quiet time, when there is nothing to do... but sew and quilt.

Beginning to Heal

by **DONNA MANN ROBERTS**
Mars Hill, North Carolina

In August of 2013 my husband, Gordon, was diagnosed with cancer. After many scans and beginning chemotherapy it was revealed that his cancer had spread throughout all of his organs. He never complained about the pain or the fact his time was limited. He was a professor at Mars Hill University, Mars Hill, North Carolina.

His concern was me and how I would get through the pain and loneliness and grief of losing him. He asked me to choose a hobby to start. After several attempts at different hobbies, I watched a YouTube of Jenny Doan demonstrating how to make a quilt. I never thought I could do this, so I picked quilting as my hobby! I love a challenge.

Gordon proceeded to dismantle his home office and build me a quilting room. I began watching every video Jenny had on YouTube. My husband passed away April 2014. With my four chihuahuas, my church family, and quilting, I am beginning to heal. It is so, so hard, but the love he had for me is in that quilting room.

Sewing in a Rocking Chair

by **CAROL BANKS CRYSTAL**
Webster City, Iowa

Back when I was younger, and that was a long time ago, we went to our grandparents' farm every summer. The day after school was out we went to the farm and the day before school started we returned to town.

This was in the day that many farms had neither running water or electricity. We would play like mad all day and after supper my grandmother would read to us by the light of a kerosene lamp. We would all pile into her lap, snuggle in, and listen. Tom Sawyer has never sounded so good.

I remember her in the rocking chair sewing postage stamp-sized blocks by hand until she had enough for a quilt for one of the beds. Each of my brothers and I have a quilt made entirely by hand; tattered and worn and oh so loved. As we grew and she had great-grandchildren, they also received hand-sewn baby quilts.

Of course our sewing machine was a treadle and she taught me to sew on it. Doll clothes were a favorite. Today I sew with my computerized machine and enjoy the process very much, but I can still see my grandmother in my memory's eye sitting in her rocker, sewing by hand. I'm sure she enjoyed it every bit as much as I. She was such a special person and is still missed by all of us.

The Best Mistake

by **FRAN MAY**
Riverton, Utah

When my three year-old grandson asked me to make him a quilt because I had made the other grandsons quilts the year before, I didn't know what kind to make. The others were into Harry Potter so I made them each a Harry Potter quilt with a matching pillowcase for those times when they had read-a-thons at school and could take a blanket and pillow. This little guy wasn't even in school.

Then I found a pattern called "There's a Monster in My Closet" and knew right away this was for him as he loved the newly released Monster's Inc. movie. I had soo much fun making it with all kinds of bright fabrics in all colors. Each monster was fussy-cut and behind a dimensional door.

I wanted to surprise him with it for Christmas and since he lives in Texas I had to get it in the mail. I had just finished quilting and binding it and started the task of clipping all the threads. As I was thus clipping, I accidentally clipped a small portion of fabric! Eek! I was mortified and

Photo Courtesy Fran May

anguished over it all night. I finally fell asleep, frustrated that I couldn't undo the mistake.

When I woke up I knew what to do! I hadn't put a label on it yet, so I made a mini door with a monster behind it, complete with a button door knob like all the others. I wrote on the label: "For my grandson, Jayden, who loves monsters. Made with all the love a grandmother can possess." Then I dated it and sent it to Texas.

When he opened it up Christmas morning he was so surprised and loved it immediately. As he began looking at it closely, he noticed all the doors opened and had all kinds of monsters behind them. Then he noticed the little door, slanted in the border and opened it see what was behind that door. His mom read the label to him and he quickly kissed the monster and said that was his "Grandma door" and it was like he could give me a kiss whenever he needed to! That became his way of giving me a bedtime kiss goodnight every night!

What started as a mistake turned out to be the best label I've ever made!

Meant to Be

by **JANICE BROUSSARD**
Katy, Texas

I made my first quilt when I was sixteen. Now as an avid quilter of almost forty years, I have received hundreds of requests to "Make me a quilt." Sometimes I will; most of the time I won't, since most non-quilters haven't a clue about the amount of work and expense that goes into a project.

When I was in my late thirties I took a Taekwondo class. The instructor was an energetic eighteen year-old young man named Will. He was home-schooled and taught the ladies' morning class. I had just finished making my five year-old daughter a matching quilt and nap mat cover for kindergarten. After class, I was showing it off and Will wrapped up in the child-sized quilt and asked me to make one for him. He went to the front desk and pulled out a piece of paper and drew me a pattern. He wanted "Mr. Smiley Face" fabric in the middle with a solid black border and he wanted yellow and black plaid fabric on the back. I told him that it had been quite some time since I had seen smiley-faced fabric, but that if I ever did, I would make him a quilt.

One week later, I was in a fabric store getting supplies for my nephew's Halloween costume. Guess what fabric was on display... Mr. Smiley Face fabric - yellow and black. One row behind that... yellow and black plaid fabric. So, I purchased enough to make a really simple quilt and made it that weekend. What else could I do?!

I gave it to Will at the next class and he was delighted. I heard that he carried it everywhere. When he spent the night with friends, so did the quilt. Road trip? Quilt. Trip to Europe with his parents? Quilt! I was happy to learn that my gift was well used.

Two years later, Will was killed in a car accident. At the funeral, the Smiley Faced quit was covering the casket. At the eulogy, his brother spoke about how much the quilt was part of his memory of his brother. I now give away a lot more quilts than I used to.

Accomplishing the Impossible

by **TERESA BRODMAN**
Upper Sandusky, Ohio

When a friend and single mom found out she was battling cancer once again, the prognosis was not good. Stacey was terminally ill and had a teenage daughter and son. She had insurance but she knew there would come a point where she could not work and receive insurance benefits, besides the insurance she had was not going to cover all the expenses. She did not want to leave her children with the burden of her medical expenses.

Her boyfriend told me he was going to have a spaghetti dinner fund-raiser for Stacey to help her with the bills. I told him I would help and might make a quilt, but the benefit was only six weeks away. Further, I was new at quilting. I had only really made an Ohio State Quilt in a class at my local sewing shop, Sew Nice. But a friend had told me I should make that quilt as a fund-raiser and I couldn't quit thinking about that quilt and Stacey.

Photo Courtesy Teresa Brodman

Stacy's children, Evan and Brittany, and Stacey Gottfried and Stacey's partner, Jerry Davidson

Knowing I that I couldn't do this on my own in under six weeks, I called five friends and asked them if they'd help me make the quilt. All of them said yes! One was an experienced quilter, one owned the local Bernina shop Sew Nice, one was a great sewer but not a quilter, there was my sister who had only taken the one quilt class with me, and my co-worker who is a good quilter. We all donated fabric from our stash. My sister couldn't help the night we pieced but cut fabric pieces for us. My co-worker Renae and I made a lot of the log cabin squares before we met to piece the quilt. We met at Sew Nice one evening and finished piecing the quilt. Heidi, the owner of Sew Nice lined up a professional quilter and got it quilted. All together, piecing the quilt and having it professionally quilted took just ten days, which totally amazed everyone! We seemed to accomplish the impossible in many ways.

Many experience quilters told us that with having that many people piece a quilt the blocks would not be the same size We did all use the same presser foot when piecing and my friend Ann, the experienced quilter, did fix a few blocks but not many. Later, when looking at that quilt, it always amazed me how perfect the quilt seemed.

We started a Facebook page called "Team Stacey" to promote the quilt and the dinner and we still use it to promote events like Relay For Life or just to say something about missing Stacey. We sold over eight thousand tickets at one for $1 or six for $5.

Stacey loved the quilt so much that she had her picture taken with it and her boyfriend Jerry and her children. It became the promotional poster for our fundraiser. Stacey died December 17, 2013 at the age of forty-five, two months after the fund-raiser.

That quilt has meant more to me than any quilt I have ever made. Although each quilt is special and given with love, this quilt showed that nothing is impossible and that together we can accomplish great things.

In a twist of irony, a Michigan Fan won the quilt, but fortunately his wife was a huge Buckeye fan.

A Passionate Life

by **JEANNE CROWELL**
Webster City, Iowa

In 1992 I moved close to my sister. She was into quilting and we took classes together by a famous quilter. I soon loved quilting as much as my sister, Carol Ann, did.

She took me to her retreats where I met many new quilters and became friends with them all. At one retreat in the woods, four of us went a day early to get more sewing in. That first night we were alone in the lodge. All of a sudden we heard a bear growling outside the sewing room window! We all froze. No one moved an inch. We thought the bear was going to come in and attack us. Finally we were able to run upstairs and lock our bedroom doors. It was scary, but fun and exciting too!

Carol Ann and I would go on weekends to different towns and shop at the local quilt shops. She was a fifth grade teacher and would tell me stories.

She was a great story teller. Every time we were together we would laugh so hard we'd cry. My sister was the greatest person I've known.

I now have a Bernina 830 and a sewing room chock full of fabric. It is my peace. Thanks all to my sister. She taught me everything she knew, which was a lot.

In 2003, Carol Ann was diagnosed with pancreatic cancer and given one year to live. She quit quilting that day. She died three months later. I was given her quilting things. I found that my sister loved to make blocks, but never finished them. She had over twenty quilts unmade.

I finished one of her quilts and gave it to my daughter. I told her it was made by my sister and me. She cried and loved it.

I miss my sister every day. Thank you Carol for teaching me to quilt. It is now my passion in life.

It Takes a Village

by **JOAN MOSTER FICHT**
Floral Park, New York

I came to know Fran Ryan when my eldest son, Michael, was in her class at our local elementary school. She was a loving, creative, and dynamic teacher and was beloved by all her students. She was well respected by her colleagues and parents alike, so when she was diagnosed with advanced stage ovarian cancer in the fall of 1997, the news shook the school community like a thunderbolt. Surely this couldn't be happening to such a young and vibrant woman who had so much to live for and to give to others. How would our children handle this news? How could we help them to understand such a painful reality? How could we best help Fran and her husband and children grasp such a difficult prognosis?

Several of us friends whose children had been in Fran's classes in recent years wanted to give the children a concrete way to offer their help and to express their affection for this special woman, so we devised a plan to have the kids create a quilt. In this way each child could take an active part in helping Mrs. Ryan to overcome seemingly unbeatable odds. Initially, this seemed a nearly impossible project as reaching out to well over a hundred past and present students would take time, organization, and a huge amount of energy. Ultimately our core group of four mothers, Joan, Arlene, Pam, and Denise, joined forces, and over the course of three and a half months our impossible task to create a quilt was accomplished.

Fran had been a stay-at-home mom for her now high-school aged children, John and Marie, for many years, and she had only returned to the classroom for the past seven years. We decided to reach out to all of her former students, as most were still in the area and could be reached via siblings or parents. Fabric was donated by a mother in the fashion industry. Fabric crayons would be easiest for the smallest hands and were bought so that even the youngest student could create something special even if that was only a simple message written on the muslin. The older students were encouraged to be more creative but always keeping in mind that positive thoughts and good wishes were most important.

We met on several nights to cut the fabric and put together packages with fabric crayons and directions to be handed to as many children as possible. We distributed these baggies to all of Fran's present and former students still in the elementary school, and reached out to the local middle/high school and parochial schools to make sure everyone had a chance to be part of "The Quilt Project". We even mailed some squares to several families who had relocated to other areas and had those blocks returned as well. Of the nearly 140 quilt blocks we distributed, we received back just over a hundred. These ranged from simple "Get well soon" words scrawled in crayon to appliquéd pictures of teachers, stuffed bears, and many, many hearts. Some were sophisticated works of art, others purely simple, but all reflected each student's love for this special woman.

Thanksgiving was our first deadline for all the squares to be returned. Denise had also created a lovely counted cross stitch picture which became the centerpiece of the quilt. Over the next three weeks, Pam and Joan sewed the quilt blocks together using a teacher-themed fabric for sashing strips. A simple muslin border was added around the edge to provide space for colleagues, parents, and friends to add their own best wishes for Fran's recovery. Our final deadline was Christmas with our dream of having the kids' quilt wrapped up lying under the Ryans' Christmas tree for Fran to discover on Christmas morning. All of us met again and tufted this "larger than king-sized" quilt to have it ready for display at the elementary school before winter break began in late December.

The response of the school community was overwhelming! There was a steady stream of parents, teachers, administrators, and friends during the day and a half before the schools closed for holiday break, everyone eager to see what the children had created and to write their own words on this special creation. Our 6 inch borders were covered with hundreds of signatures and good wishes for Fran's speedy recovery, and the rainbow of colors in the blocks captivated all who came to see our "miracle" quilt. It was the talk of the building, the district, and in much of the neighborhood. Could this simple expression help to stem the tide of the cancer?

As planned, the large box holding the hearts of all who were part of this project was discovered under the Ryans' tree on Christmas morning. Fran, although weakened by weeks of chemotherapy and its side effects, was amazed at her gift and promptly spent the day wrapped up in hugs of all of her students and friends. When her cancer went into remission the following February, Fran returned to the classroom with her creative energy intact to the joy of her students and their parents.

We'll never truly know just how much that miracle quilt contributed to Fran's healing. The medical community is only now beginning to recognize the effect that prayer and meditation have on illness, but I know with all certainty that all those prayers and good wishes wrapped in that quilt helped to give Fran the eighteen months of good health she enjoyed. Sadly she succumbed to the cancer in May of 1999, able to spend almost all of those days in her classroom.

The Quilt That Made an Impression

by **CLAIRE MILLER**
Glen Burnie, Maryland

I was maybe thirty-eight or so and working. My dearest friend, Sharon, had been a quilter for many, many years and while younger than I was, we just played well together. She taught beginning quilting.

This was WAY before rotary cutters and all the fancy stuff that now makes it so easy. So sitting on the floor by the copy machine with cardboard, standard rule, pencil, and scissors she proceeded to teach me to make templates. From there we cut out fabric pieces using scissors. She taught me one block at a time leading me through a sampler quilt.

Ben Franklin fabric, ninety-nine cents a yard, was all I could afford. Once I finished my blocks Sharon showed me how to set them in a pattern and how to sew them together. Well, I just got carried away with my blocks and when it came time to put a border on it, the top was so big that Sharon took it home with her because I never would have been able to do it. Can you say, "bigger than king size"?!

We pinned the layers together and turned it inside out and then pinned it again to prepare it to be hand tied. My daughter was to be married and I really wanted this quilt to be perfect. I put my whole heart into this quilt. Did I mention I did a lot of pinning to hold it together inside out?

Well, after sewing the edges and leaving the opening to turn it, I removed all the pins, turned it inside out and pressed it out. It was lopsided and had many, many wrinkles that were sewn over and other little blips. Finally it was sewn, turned, re-pinned and then hand tied.

I was totally proud of my very first quilt that was actually larger than a king size bed. I folded it neatly (sorta) and presented it to my sweet daughter and son-in-law.

I did mention that I really pinned it a lot, right? The first night they used it, they got so many pin scratches on them, the quilt actually drew blood! My son-in-law used needle-nose pliers to remove the pins that were buried inside the fabric.

My daughter and her husband continued to use that homemade quilt for years and years and then my two granddaughters carried it everywhere: to sleepovers, the beach, etc. This quilt gave us so many hysterically funny moments that it's by far the best quilt I have ever made.

I am now moving close to seventy-one and this is the happiest quilt that I have ever made. Because there was so much love and enthusiasm in it, it remains a favorite part of their love story.

My beloved daughter passed recently, but there are still tatters of that quilt folded up in their home today.

Finding the New Me

by **BARBARA GRACE**
Burlington, Maine

I made my first quilt when I was engaged to be married. That was over twenty years ago. I've made countless quilts since then. I worked slowly and deliberately trying to make each quilt a work of art. I have loved each stage of the quilting process from shopping for fabrics to selecting patterns to sewing that final binding stitch. I get a little thrill just from looking at a stack of fabric read to be cut. The possibilities are endless.

I never realized how important quilting was to me until I lost it. Two years ago I started work on a new quilt for my thirteen year old daughter. She was ready to redecorate her room with a more sophisticated style and the quilt would be the inspiration piece for the entire room. I selected the window pane pattern and purchased a dizzying array of fabrics in teal, white, and black. I got through the cutting stage and made a few sample blocks. Then, disaster struck - quite literally.

At forty-eight years old, I suffered a brain aneurysm. In just one moment, my entire life changed. Quilting was the furthest thing from my mind; I was fighting to survive. The odds were against me. Over sixty percent of patients who have a bleeding brain aneurysm die before they make it to the hospital. Of those who make it, more than fifty percent suffer major deficits that affect their quality of life dramatically. I was lucky. I lived. Recovery was slow and painful. Worse still, as soon as I recovered from this initial onslaught, I was scheduled for a second, more invasive brain surgery. Doctors had discovered two additional aneurysms in my brain that had to be removed before they too started to bleed.

My surgeries were successful. I recovered, slowly regaining strength and balance and fine motor skills. My vision, however, was severely impacted. The aneurysm damaged a nerve behind my right eye. I had double vision and my depth perception was terrible as evidenced by my frequent collisions with doorways, counters and chairs. A third surgery on my eyes helped, and again I began the slow recovery process.

My daughter's quilt was shoved to the back of a closet, a messy pile of teal and black squares with white strips snaking through them.

Life moves on. My daughter went back to school and my husband to work, and I found myself alone at home. I could not drive or work. Television and reading gave me headaches. What could I do with my time? One day I spied those fabric squares in a bag in the closet. Could I focus enough to sew? Could I even thread the needle? I was glad the

Photo Courtesy Barbara Grace

cutting was done since I did not trust myself with a blade. Never one to waste good fabric, I thought I'd give it a try.

Surprisingly, I found that concentrating my vision on that one small area under my needle helped me to focus. Threading the needle was hard but with glasses and a piece of white paper for contrast, I could do it.

Slowly, the quilt started to take shape. As it grew, so did my confidence. As it became something new, I found a new me. I am not the same as I was before and I never will be, but I have come to understand that different is not worse. Like a quilt, I was taken apart. Little pieces of me were scattered around, and slowly I had to put myself together again.

I finished the quilt in time for my daughter's fifteenth birthday. It was eighteen months since I started it.

Since then, I have completed many more quilts. I work differently now - faster and with a greater sense of joy. I scour the Missouri Star Quilt site - I think I have watched every one of your tutorials! I am always on the lookout for fun fabrics and I take advantage of Missouri Star's daily deals knowing that the quilt they will someday become will reveal itself to me to me in due time.

My quilts helped me recreate myself. As I stitched them together, I put my own life back together. I find a quiet joy in each quilt I make. I am grateful that I can create something beautiful that will last long after I am gone.

Crying, Cursing, and Quilting

by **NICOL SARGENT**
Naples, Florida

Why do I quilt? My husband died. It's that simple. As I was cleaning out his closet and getting ready to donate his clothes to a local Catholic charity, I was looking at all of his beautiful shirts and reminiscing where he had worn each one.

Living in a small community, I just could not bear the thought of seeing someone walking down the street wearing one of his shirts. A very good friend of mine, Jessica Stewart, had recently opened a small quilting shop called Ginger Threads. As I followed her on Facebook and watched some of the lovely things she created in her shop, a thought took hold. Why not take my husband's shirts and make a quilt? Then another thought took hold. I don't know how to make a quilt.

With Jessica's guidance, I began the process. I cut the shirts apart and cried. I ironed stabilizer to the material and cried. I cut blocks and cried. I sewed blocks and cried. I ripped seams and cried. And then I cursed. I ironed and cursed, cut and cursed, sewed and cursed, and ripped seams and cursed. But along the way, as I sewed each block together, I

Photo Courtesy Nicol Sargent

remembered all the happy times that we had together. My quilt became a sort of therapy for me.

And now my quilt is finished. It's far from perfect. It would never win even an honorable mention. But it's mine. It's made with love, the same love that I had for my husband. And at night, I lay it over the top of me, and it is like I can feel his arms around me once again.

I have continued to quilt because I found that I rather enjoy it. My work is still far from perfect, but only I know where the mistakes are, and the recipients of my quilts know that they are loved as well because of the time and expense in each one. Quilting has given me something to fill my days and nights with. I have always believed the saying - busy hands and an idle mind. Quilting to me continues to be a therapy of sorts. I still think about my husband daily and I think he would be proud of what I've accomplished. That's why I quilt.

What I've Gained

by **CARMEN BROKER**
Dover, Pennsylvania

Quilting has become my vacation at home. I can quickly forget about everything else going on in my life while I quilt. I am thirtytwo years old; I have a loving husband, a three and a half year old son named Connor, and a spunky one and a half year old daughter named Peyton.

Back when Peyton was only two weeks old, I was diagnosed with Stage 3c breast cancer. Despite a year full of treatments and surgeries, after Peyton's first birthday I was ultimately diagnosed as Stage 4 with the cancer spreading to my brain, lungs, lymph nodes, and liver. I was given two to three years to live. It was shortly after I was recovering from the stage 4 news that an angel named Susan lovingly offered to show me how to quilt. It could not have come at a better time.

I believe that Susan and quilting were sent to me as gifts at a time when I needed them the most.

Last November I wanted to make family Christmas stockings. I was pretty sure I knew what I was doing, but I'm always up for good tips so I checked out some instructional videos on Youtube. I browsed a few videos, most were a bit boring or very slow until I found one by Missouri Star Quilt Company, with a woman that made me think, "I would love to sew with her!"

Once completed, I posted my project on Facebook, and soon after a friend named Susan asked me if I wanted to quilt. I responded with "I don't think I can do that!" She offered to drive up from another state for a day and show me, and I was instantly excited. Little did I know what I was getting into!

Two weeks later, Susan drove the two hours to my house and brought me fabric, supplies, and spent the day with me as I finished my first quilt top from a charm pack. I was blown away by the precut options, rotary cutters, mats, rulers, and what really made quilting doable for me was learning about "nesting the seams". I had so much fun that day!

I knew I was meant to quilt when Susan said, "Oh, by the way, you have got to check out this Daily Deal thing on a website called Missouri Star Quilt Company." I quickly said, "OMG, I watched one of her videos and I just love her!!!" I took it as a sign!

I made my next quilt top all on my own, a large quilt out of a jelly roll. I had it ready to quilt by the time Susan made it back to see me. She

Photo Courtesy Carmen Broiker

said her gift to me was to take it to a long arm quilter and have it professionally finished. I was thrilled! I saw then this was going to be a serious hobby and my dining room table was not going to cut it.

Fortunately, I have a small front living room that we hardly used that I was able to turn into my quilting room. I just love it. When Susan comes over, we buckle down! My mom helps with my children and I sew and sew as Susan irons, cuts, and watches the pattern. We barely stop to eat! Susan quickly became a close friend that somehow knew what to say or not to say if I started to tear up randomly.

It didn't take me long to notice another reason I love to quilt. I am essentially using a power tool to stab something hundreds to thousands of times! Ha ha! I wonder if anyone else has noticed this? Either way, I make a funny mental note to "keep an eye on this one" when I meet someone new who likes to quilt! I bet we all have something we need to stab out of our systems!

My aunt developed ovarian cancer last October. She lives in Germany, so I hardly get to see her. I am about to start on her quilt, so she will have something to treasure and give her comfort.

There is a chance that my children won't remember me beyond stories and pictures, but they will have several quilts from me to hold. As a mother, I want to exist as much as I can for my family. I think this is true for most quilters; we want to make something to be remembered by.

I had to give up my career, my hair, and much more to battle cancer. It is so nice to have gained quilting as something for ME to enjoy. The fact that it is also a way to "hug" my loved ones makes it even better.

I hope and pray I live long enough to teach many others how to quilt and pay the quilt love forward!

Priorities

by **SARA JO COLLINS**
Cabool, Missouri

On December 7, 2010, while driving to work, I had a terrible wreck. I had just purchased my first brand new car and had recently paid it off. After the wreck, I came to while the On Star lady was speaking to me and asking if I could hear her. She let me know that help was on the way.

A passing motorist, who also happened to be a neighbor, checked on me and took off in a flash to notify my husband, Larry. The neighbor knew that Larry would be milking cows in the barn and would not be able to hear the phone. One of the people on my call list through On Star was my son, Adam. As the ambulance arrived and my husband and son arrived at the scene, the attendants began stabilizing and assessing my situation. They let me know they would be taking me to the hospital.

As they began to load me into the ambulance, I looked up at my son and said, "Don't forget to get my Tonga Treats out of the car." The ambulance attendants quickly asked, " What? What is she saying?" My son rolled his eyes and said, "That's her new quilt fabric. SHE'S GOING TO BE FINE!"

Stitches That Mend

by **AMANDA**
Australia

I am a mother of three wonderful sons. Is there any other kind? One of my sons really has been special, and has taken a lot more thought and meditation. You know those boys who get into trouble constantly, despite half the time they weren't in the wrong? They just have a love of life and curiosity that is wonderful to behold yet wears you out at the same time. The boisterous kind that everyone laughs at but secretly thanks the universe that THEIR child isn't like that?

He is also the boy with the kindest heart of my three, who would give anyone his treat if he saw they didn't have some. He was the boy who would spend hours dancing or coloring with our friend's down syndrome girl when we had her to stay. But that didn't stop people judging him harshly.

He went off the rails in a huge way when he hit his teens and caused me no end of grief, worry, and tears. I cry every time I remember this difficult time in our lives. It culminated in him leaving home at the tender age of sixteen.

He moved from just outside a little country town in regional Australia to another state far away from me. I used to lay awake at night during winter, worrying if he was warm enough. So my first quilt was for him, made with mother's love to keep him warm and safe away from me.

When he took delivery of it, he boasted to a dear friend of mine "See how much work my mum has put into this for me (the same mum he hated for being strict and wanting him safe). See how perfect the stitching is (it wasn't). I thought that it would be an old granny quilt, but this is the best!

That quilt played a big part in mending our relationship and that is what quilts are for me. They are something to keep your family safe and warm, so that they know their mother, sister, and daughter loves them.

I Knew I Could Do It

by **RINA MASON**
Adrian, MO

I was born with a rare birth defect and spent at least two months out of every year from age five to twenty-five in the hospital undergoing surgeries and procedures. Since I couldn't interact with other children for months at a time I taught myself to sew at the age of ten. I loved creating my own clothes as I couldn't purchase off the rack because everything needed to be altered to fit my birth defect.

When I was seventeen my mother saw a picture of a sampler quilt and asked if I could make one for her. I had never made a quilt but knew I could do it. I hand pieced it and hand quilted it and from that moment on I was hooked. I could take my squares and triangles to the hospital with me and have something to keep me occupied for the long hospitalizations. Not only did the hand piecing and quilting take my mind off the hospital stays, but the nurses and doctors loved watching my quilts come together. As a matter of fact, I was hospitalized last month and took my fabric, cutting mat, rotary cutter, needle and thread with me. I think every nurse came in to see my progress, and I met quite a few who were quilters.

My birth defect causes constant pain and I soon found out that sewing took my mind off the pain, and I didn't have to rely on pain medications so much. I have been quilting for over forty years and spend some time every day at my machine. While I'm quilting I am so engrossed in the planning, cutting, and sewing that most of the time I can ignore the pain and all the complications that accompany my problem. The hum of the machine and the rhythm of the needle going up and down is music to my soul. It's better therapy than any doctor could prescribe. Quilting also leads to new experiences and new friends which in turn brings laughter and wonderful memories into my life.

I am convinced that quilting is one of the reasons that I am still alive, as I was told that no one with my birth defect survives past eighteen and I'm now sixty-two. I may not be in the best shape, but I get up everyday looking forward to reading quilting blogs, discovering new patterns, making new quilts, going to quilt shops, and enjoying the company of other quilters.

I fully intend to keep quilting for the next thirty or so years and prove the doctors wrong because there are just too many quilts waiting to be made.

First Impressions

by **ANGELIKA PURVIS**
Copperas Cove, Texas

My husband, Fred, and I met in 1981 on Christmas Eve, and by 1983 we decided to try our life together. Fred was in the Army and got a transfer back to the States. We both wanted to make sure that I would be happy, and we planned a stay with his parents in Owingsville, Kentucky to learn a little more about the country I was moving to.

After a long flight from Germany, my husband picked me up in Lexington and drove us to his parents house. The welcome I received was just overwhelming, and after some pleasant talk I wanted to rest for the night. My then soon-to-be mother-in-law showed me to my room. I just saw the bed and crashed. When I woke up the next morning the first thing I noticed was a "blanket" with so many different pieces of fabric, I just had to ask my husband why he did not tell me that his parents were so poor to have rags on the bed.

Well, my future mother-in-law heard my conversation, and later in the day she asked me to escort her back to the room. My heart fell down so hard to the floor that she must have heard this. She explained to me that the quilt on the bed (she did not call it a blanket) was made out clothing pieces from Fred and his three siblings as a memory to remember them growing up. She had placed this quilt especially on the bed to welcome me to the family.

I think that the kindness she showed me at the day was giving me a chance to remember that the first look should not be the last.

That May in 1983, the days had plenty of gray clouds on the sky, and rain was almost a daily occurrence. Hildred, Fred's mother, gave me my first sewing lesson and I have made many quilts since then. As long as she was with us I made it my goal to make sure a picture of every quilt or ribbon would make the trip to Kentucky. She was not only the inspiration to start quilting, she still is my inspiration.

My husband can only blame his mother if I spend too much time on my sewing machine or working out the plans for another quilt, or if just have to go on the internet and order me some more fabric.

Saved by Quilting

by **JILL FISHER, PIE LADY QUILTS**
Iowa City, Iowa

Quilting saved me. I don't remember much from that dark day in Labor and Delivery, but I do remember the nurse apologizing because she didn't have a quilt to give me, not as some kind of horrible consolation prize, but as a tangible memory of the baby girl we had lost. "We never have enough quilts," she said with regret. I was a broken woman, drowning in grief, my entire world upended, and she had unknowingly thrown me a life preserver. She had given me a purpose.

I went home and turned my hobby into my passion. In the soft early morning light, while my house and its occupants slept, I turned to the sewing room for comfort. I found that I liked the solitude. I craved the peace I found in the simple repetitive tasks of cutting, pressing, and sewing. Being around people and platitudes was hard for me, but my sewing machine could murmur soft and soothing words to my soul. I made stillborn blanket after stillborn blanket in those quiet hours. I stitched and I cried until I was out of tears. I stitched together fabric and the pieces of my broken heart until I felt whole once more.

Photo Courtesy Jill Fisher

Soon I was pregnant again and when I felt the weight of worry crushing the breath out of me, I turned to the sewing machine for relief. I stitched and counted kicks and stitched again. I let the sewing machine murmur to both of us. I put the stillborn blankets aside and worked instead on making blankets for my boys. Having faced my demon, I wanted to focus on creation and love. I wanted my boys to fall asleep wrapped in my love for them. I needed my daughter to grow and develop in an environment without fear or worry.

Once that sweet little girl was born, she became my alarm clock for an even earlier morning. After her feeding, she would settle for another few hours of peaceful sleep and I would fly down the stairs in my nightgown and bare feet to sew some more. What I lost in sleep, I gained in well-being. One of her first words was "pretty." I watched her gaze at the quilts hanging on the wall, turn to me with a 4-tooth gummy smile and say "pitty." She is a gift to me in many ways. I always want my children to associate their mother with light and color and beautiful things.

I still get up early. An hour or two with my right-brain in charge positively impacts my entire day. Once my children wake up, I can be a devoted mama with love and time to freely give. While they sleep, the schedules, routines, and to-do lists fade, and I let my instincts take over. For those few hours I let color and texture and line come to the forefront and I become a maker in a different sense. Having a creative outlet gives me peace. Quilting is that outlet.

When I joined the online community, quilting became my voice. I formed meaningful relationships and connected with like-minded people from all over the world—kind, generous people who also share a passion for creating beautiful things. I have grown as I have shared my work and studied the work of others. I have received so many warm gestures of friendship that I have become a better friend.

The path to creativity and contentment is different for every person. I have found mine. Quilting has trained my eyes to see the beauty in life, and it is everywhere.

I am proud to be a quilter.

A Gift From My Husband

by **CATHY HOWE**
Mason, Ohio

Quilting was a gift from my husband, but even he would be amazed at how it has "saved" me.

Not too long after we were married, I noticed an ad for a beginning quilting class near my office. Michael knew I wanted to learn more about the craft my grandmother tried to teach me when I was much younger, so he insisted I take the class. From that point on I was hooked.

Two years and two cheap sewing machines later, Michael gave me a far-too-expensive quilting machine for Christmas. "A proper craftsman needs proper tools," he reasoned.

That argument held fast when he purchased a wooden quilting frame for me. He lovingly stained the frame so it would last longer, he claimed. He proudly escorted folks who came to visit into the sewing room to see the frame and how it worked.

Photo Courtesy Cathy Howe

I never felt like I had to sneak any fabric purchases into the house or store fabric in appliances like some quilters do. Michael loved to see my purchases and projects and hear my plans. He'd attend quilt shows with me for two reasons: to flirt with the other quilters and to find things he could use for his own hobby.

Michael was a model railroader with a far more expensive hobby. Perhaps he reasoned that if my quilting took up more of my time, he wouldn't feel so guilty over all the hours he spent tinkering with his trains. His train room was at one end of the house and my sewing room at the other. He often joked we never saw much of each other.

Michael was diagnosed with pulmonary fibrosis six years ago. The disease robbed him of the ability to breathe unaided. His oxygen tubes trailed throughout the house to the train room and the sewing room. He was still involved with my quilting, advising me on colors, patterns and fabric storage. His youngest daughter was getting married and he insisted on selecting the pattern, the fabrics, and even the quilting design. When his grand-daughter announced her engagement, their wedding quilt had to be made with bright, tropical colors, he insisted. Each quilt had his stamp of approval before being mailed to their new owners. Eventually, those quilt "shows" were confined to his bedroom, no longer able to walk even with the oxygen tanks/tubes.

"When I'm gone," he said one evening, "You can have the train room for your sewing room. It's much bigger." I replied that I didn't want to talk about it.

Two days later he was gone.

My son helped me honor Michael's last wishes by making the train room into a beautiful sewing room. I feel Michael's presence in that room. Perhaps it's because he spent so many hours in there. There are times I sit in that room, doing nothing in particular, but feeling more at ease there than any place in the world.

And how did all this save me? I handled my grief through quilting. I made quilts for each of Michael's hospice aides, comfort quilts for friends facing losses of their own, and gifts. Since his passing, I've created a special quilt each year for hospice to raffle for their fundraising. I can never, ever repay that organization for all the loving care they gave Michael and my family.

As my quilting skills improved, I pushed myself to meet other quilters, make new friends, attend shows, and enjoy weekend retreats. It's been my window to the world as life goes on. Quilting is not just a hobby for me; it has become a way of life.

I now have loads of projects in various stages of construction and a room packed with fabric, thread, tools, books, and patterns. I have become a confident quilter. Yet, there are times when I question my choices...

If I ever doubt my color selection for a new project, I can hear Michael say, "That color is bloody awful, try another."

And it makes me smile.

From the Heart

by **JACKIE MANTON**
Topsham, Maine

A little boy in my granddaughter's third-grade class had brain cancer. The treatment required multiple surgeries. During one surgery, his optic nerve was nicked and the little boy was blinded. His class at school wanted to make him a quilt so that when he came back to school, he could cover up in his wheelchair and go outside during recess and be warm. My granddaughter volunteered me to help. The teacher, having never quilted, emailed me with her thoughts of doing a tied fleece blanket. When the teacher and I finally got together to plan the event, I made a suggestion. Children are remarkably imaginative, so "let's give them a chance to create their own masterpiece," I said.

I brought 8" muslin squares to school, along with different types of fabric and every bead, button, ribbon, bric-brac, pom-pom, and every other embellishment I had (which was substantial). The kids designed their own squares, cut out shapes from fabrics that had different textures, and sewed them by hand onto muslin. My job was to thread needles and put the squares together. We spent every afternoon for a week sewing. It was truly a masterpiece.

Nowhere have I ever seen a more beautiful quilt. One block was the shape of a horse cut from fur. Jute was braided and sewn to the horse neck for its reins. On another block, fabric was cut in the shape of a phone with buttons added for numbers, and a padded hand receiver attached with elastic. The kids made fire engines with sequined tires, clowns with big soft pom-pom noses and button eyes, playground equipment with strings and felt; you name it and it was probably on the quilt. I went to Build-a-Bear and purchased sound chips for them to embed in a few of the blocks. They recorded sounds and songs on blank chips. That wasn't quite enough for them. They wanted to autograph their blocks. I explained that their friend couldn't read anymore. So I added sashing to the bottom of each block and used floss and French knots to put the name of the child who made each block in Braille.

I was not at the school when the little boy came back and received the quilt. However, I heard that his mom cried during the presentation and that the boy used it every day. The children felt a great sense of accomplishment and pride, especially when they had fun on the playground at recess with him. When some of the teachers later mentioned to me that I did a wonderful job making the quilt, I had to tell them "I did not make the quilt, talk to the kids about it."

My granddaughter graduates from high school this year and still speaks of that quilt. Those kids will likely never forget that project.

Why do I quilt? Because those children so touched my heart.

I do a lot of charity quilting. My quilts go to a local hospital, the state children's cancer unit, a school for kids with behavioral issues, and on and on. I hope my quilts touch the lives of these children the way that third grade class touched my life.

My Friend Jenny

by **NANCY L. ROBINSON**
Stoddard, New Hampshire

I am a member of the Cheshire Quilters Guild, Keene, NH and a subgroup that meets every Wednesday. My quilting girlfriend, Jo-Anne, introduced me to your website. I loved the daily deal and the stories immediately. I binge-watched the videos! I loved the shortcuts, tips and tricks you demonstrated to simplify otherwise complicated piecing. My head buzzed with the new variety of patterns that I could confidently execute and share with the guild members.

At the next weekly sewing session as soon as I arrived, I announced to the group that they just had to watch this video which simplified making half-square triangles that "My friend Jenny" posted on her website. Jo-Anne's jaw dropped, her eyebrows raised and she questioned... "Your friend Jenny?" and we started to laugh. She explained to the other ladies that she had just recently introduced me to the Missouri Star website, and my enthusiasm for and bonding with my “new friend” was rather sudden. We all laughed and agreed that if Jenny lived closer she would fit right into our quilters’ group. Now when we regularly share ideas, patterns, or tips with each other, they tease me saying, “Did you get that idea from YOUR friend, Jenny?” Although distance separates us, Jenny and I are BQFFs (Best Quilting Friends Forever), because I have declared it!

Your BQFF,

Nancy

I Quilt Instead

by **SHENA ALEXANDER**
Apo, AE

My husband is a pilot in the United States Air Force. I'm so proud of him, his sacrifice, and his service, but it does make for some horribly lonely moments. We have been married for five years and during that time he's been away (sometimes thousands of miles away in a war zone) for approximately half of it. Most of my time is spent raising my sweet precious children, but I needed something that was just mine.

My mom quilts, my grandma quilts, and even my great-grandma quilted... so I guess the passion for quilting was in my blood before I even knew it.

About a year ago, I complained to my mom (back in the States in Missouri) that I was really struggling with anxiety and fear during the evenings after my boys went to bed and I was home, while my husband

Photo Courtesy Shena Alexander

was away fighting one of our many wars. She suggested I take up sewing. So, I did! That very night, I ordered a sewing machine and all the necessities, fabric, and thread. Before my machine even arrived (mail takes a while here in Italy sometimes), I started watching the Jenny MSQC tutorials. I was so excited to try all these techniques and make quilts!

Fast forward a year. I have set up an entire room in my house for sewing, I've created a few quilts and so many more fun little side projects! I have stacks of fabric and templates and so many ideas about what to sew next!

So, why do I quilt? Instead of worrying about all the what-ifs that could happen in my husband's job, I quilt. Instead of being lonely for months on end, I mark my days by all the progress made on my latest quilting project. Instead of feeling sorry for myself, I quilt creations for loved ones. My husband leaves in a week for a six-month deployment, and instead of tearing up thinking about it, I walk into my sewing room, excited about my stacks of fabric and what I will create next. That's why I quilt.

Quilting to Recovery

by **L.E.W.**
Hagerstown, Maryland

When I was 26 years old, I was diagnosed with Lyme Disease. It was bad. I had been misdiagnosed several times as having five or six different things, and my Lyme had gone untreated (or mistreated) for nine years. I had become so ill that, upon my diagnosis, I had to resign from my job and go into a rigorous treatment, unsure if I could ever go back to doing the work that I love: teaching special needs students.

After a few months unable to get out of bed, I could finally sit up. I couldn't read (my eyes and brain wouldn't permit it), and the television gave me a headache. My mother discovered a pile of fabric and suggested that I "make something pretty." She hauled out my grandmother's 1950's Singer machine that had hung, unused, in its table since she had died. I was supplied with extra pillows and my grandmother's sewing box and left to my own devices. Despite the pain in my hands, I began cutting squares and I found that the more I cut, the better my hands felt. I began arranging squares and found that the more I had something for my brain to work on, the better it felt too.

When I was finished with my quilt top, it was hideous and crooked, but I was so pleased that I was able to do something besides lay in bed that I began listening to the audio from YouTube quilt tutorials (I still couldn't handle the screen). I learned the wonders of *gasp* seam allowances, chain piecing, and using an IRON (Jenny Doan even taught me to make my own ironing board!) YouTube tutorials became my constant companion while in recovery. Eventually I was even able to go pick out my own fabric! I quilted myself right into recovery.

It's five years later. I have been in symptom management for three of those years (that means I'm much better.) I've taught my mother to quilt, and she's retiring this year and starting her own quilt company. To top it all off, I'm writing this during my lunch break at work, finally able to be back in the classroom teaching math and science to middle and high-schoolers with moderate to severe disabilities. I also have fabric waiting in my sewing room for when I get home (it's a double wedding ring table runner).

Quilting kept my mind sharp when I thought I would lose it, my hands strong when everything felt so weak, and it gave me something to look forward to and plan for... and I plan on quilting until I can't quilt anymore.

If You Want Something Quilted Right, Quilt It Yourself!

by **VONNA MCKOY**
Augusta, Georgia

Quilter is a term I recently added to my repertoire of mom, wife, and grandmother. While I like to dabble in 'do-it-yourself' projects, sewing was one I felt was beyond my reach.

After successfully becoming pregnant, my daughter announced that she wanted a quilt for her baby daughter. She even went on the various websites and found a pattern she liked in her favorite colors: purple, accented with yellow and gray.

Determined to keep my status of "SHEro," the feminist hero in her life, I immediately set out to find someone to sew this quilt for me to give to her as a baby shower gift. Little did I know the task of purchasing such an item would prove to be more daunting than anticipated. I asked a few friends who quilted quite well but was told "no" on multiple occasions with humble responses that they didn't quilt very well. I found out soon after that my daughter was also on a mission to get her daughter a quilt too but was equally unsuccessful as I in getting the task done.

Photo Courtesy Vonna McKoy

With eight weeks left to the baby shower deadline, I took to the internet in the hopes of purchasing a quilt. I found a wonderful store online and sent a picture of the quilt we hoped to receive. After assurance that the quilt could be duplicated in pattern with different material I decided to not only purchase the quilt but an entire bedding set. Upon receiving the items five weeks later I was very surprised when all the items appeared as described in the order with the exception of the quilt. Multiple emails resulted in the vendor indicating she could not duplicate the item.

With two weeks left to the baby shower, I was more determined than ever. I went to my storage closet pulled out a sewing machine I purchased seven years ago and immediately Googled "how to make a baby quilt." To my surprise I was taken to a YouTube video by Missouri Star Quilt Co. titled "Disappearing Nine Patch." After watching the video several times I went out the next day and purchased fabric.

When I discussed the pending project with my spouse he responded, "You don't sew, don't waste the material. Find someone else to do it." Hearing this made me want to make it even more. I went to the internet again, found my sewing machine make and model and Googled "how to thread the machine" and "how to make a bobbin." As the day of the baby shower loomed closer, the naysayers began to increase. All my friends, coworkers, and family (including my husband) continued to tell me to give up the task. Instead I watched the "Disappearing Nine Patch" video and became more determined.

Instead of the finished product being a baby quilt it actually grew bigger and bigger as I added different borders and designs from other videos I liked from the website. Needless to say, I was laughed at repeatedly about it not being a baby quilt. I am very pleased to say that not only did I complete the quilt on time in a personal record of eight days, but my daughter loves it so much she wants to keep it for herself. She was truly surprised at the baby shower and could not believe I sewed it for Valerie. She even loves the large size and says Valerie will take it to college someday.

Photo Courtesy Vonna McKoy

As for the naysayers, they have all apologized and were very shocked that I was not only able to accomplish the task but it turned out fabulous. I am proud to say I have now been quilting for seven months and have made six other quilts and two pillows.

Today, I still refer to myself as a quilter when people ask me if I sew. I have just started a quilting club here in Okinawa, Japan, and yes, we are all beginners. They have all recently purchased sewing machines and we are having a sleepover soon in which I will teach them how to thread their machines and make bobbins. Thank you for making quilting easy and fun through your many tutorial videos. I am forever thankful for the Missouri Star Quilt Co. tutorials and look forward to sharing the website with the group.

Free At Last!

by **NANCY W. RHODEN**
Frisco, Texas

At sixty-one years old I fell in love for the second time. After fifteen years of being single, the new marriage satisfied my need for companionship. It was a such a blessing. We spent every moment together.

Of course we watched TV and the remote naturally turned to sports. All the time sports! All the time! I soon realized I knew who the quarterbacks were for the pro football teams. How could I have slipped so far into the abyss? Scary!! I had to claw my way out!

I needed a hobby. I had always sewed and wanted to quilt. My internet research led me to Missouri Star and I studied, watching the tutorials. My first quilt was nothing to brag about, but I got better. I learned the tricks and applied the tips.

Photo Courtesy Nancy W. Rhoden

In 2013 I made thirteen pieced tops of children themed fabric and sent them to an orphanage we support in Haiti. Because it is hot there I could not add batting but only a backing. As I finished each sheet I prayed for the children. Each sheet had a tiny cross made of white buttons, and I included toys that matched each "play sheet." Our friends went to Haiti and took the treasures. The children were thrilled! It was such a labor of love! It was a far better use of my time than football watching.

The best news is: I have been healed... I could not tell you a single quarterback's name! Praise God... free at last, free at last!

Oh no, he has turned the TV to golf. I must escape to my sewing room!

Smiling From Heaven

by **SUE FRUIA**
Laredo, Texas

In 1985 I gave birth to a beautiful baby boy. My husband and I named him Lucas. He was to be the first male born in my husband's family in twenty-six years. We planned for everything. His room was beautiful and made ready for his coming home. The only problem was he was never coming home. My beautiful son died from cord complications. When they brought my baby to me to see him for the first time, he was wrapped in a paper blanket. That paper blanket is etched in my mind. I will never forget that blue paper blanket.

When I arrived home my daughter asked where was our baby. I explain that he was with God and someday we will get to see him. My son was buried in his coming home clothes and his service was private. I couldn't face people.

Time passed and I still found myself thinking of that paper blanket. It was then that I decided to take quilting lessons. I come from a town in the southernmost part of Texas. Everybody I asked about quilting classes kept saying that none were available. It took twentyeight years before I could take lessons. I watched Missouri Star quilting videos and I improved my quilting skills. Now I make life quilts for babies that are born to new parents. I celebrate my son with quilts. I recently went to visit his grave and told him about my quilts. I actually felt better and I knew he was smiling from heaven.

Time for a Party!

by **KELLY DEPALMA**
Stoneboro, Pennsylvania

I have been quilting for twenty years. My loving husband, Dan, has always been so supportive in my addiction! I was able to go to a quilting retreat early on when my children were four and six. He decided to make it great fun for the girls for the weekend, and promised them they would rent movies and get popcorn, snacks, junk food, etc.

I left Friday morning for the retreat and Dan took the girls to the grocery store to stock up on all the goodies and movies. As they were checking out the cashier said, “My my, it looks like you all are going to have a good time tonight.” My four year-old responded with “We are! Our mommy left, and Daddy says we can have a party!”

Well, talk about a red face on my husband’s part! He was almost stuttering trying to explain to the clerk what she meant. I still laugh about it, and have shared it with the retreat ladies many times. I just went for my twentieth retreat this past January and I LOVE it!

A Worldwide Quilting Circle

by **ZULFIYA BRAYLO**
Ufa, Russia

I fell in love with quilting as a little girl. I remember visiting relatives in the countryside of Safarovo, Russia. They had beautiful handmade quilts that I could spend hours contemplating. As I later found out, they had a beautiful tradition when a woman passed away, they would tear the fabric and give pieces to the women in the community, her friends and neighbors. Those women made quilts using the fabrics. So every quilt had lots of stories to tell of all those women of Safarovo.

When I was about three or four years old I remember playing with scissors and cutting fabric in the house, including pillowcases. My mom saw my curiosity and love of fabrics and before I knew it she brought home little pieces of fabrics from a friend that was working at the tailor shop. My mom gave me a needle and thread and thought me how to do simple stitches. I'm so grateful to my mom that she was able to recognize my desire and help me to learn how to sew.

I never would have thought that the magic of fabric would change my life. When I was working at a custom tailor shop, I couldn't help but

Photo Courtesy Zulfiya Braylo

save all the little pieces of leftover fabric and started experimenting with quilting. In 2011 I made a quilt for a Russian quilting competition. It had elements of traditional tartar embroidery patterns and appliquéd ornaments. It was very special to my heart because it reflected my love for my heritage. Although my cat had an accident on the quilt and I had to spend several hours using soap and a fan to clean the mess, I was able to get first place!

I love how quilting makes me want to move forward and stay positive when things are not looking so hot in my life. Quilting helps me to communicate love and warmth to my loved ones. It also helps me to see beauty and I see the world differently because of quilting. It helps me to stay young and happy!

The List

by **KRISTIN BEASLEY**
Cushing, Oklahoma

When I turned thirty I made a list. At the top of the page I wrote, "If I Don't Do These Things by the Time I'm Fifty, I'll Be Mad At Myself." (I am not great at titles. Also, I am wordy.) Number one on the list? Make a quilt.

I confess, in hindsight, I'm not really sure where that came from. I come from a long line of women who sew, but I had never sewn a stitch. I didn't even own a sewing machine. But I had always been drawn to fabric and quilts, and something about turning thirty sparked a desire in me to try my hand at making my own.

I have read stories of people who decided to make a quilt, bought some fabric and a sewing machine, and just started sewing. I am not quite so brave. I borrowed my grandmother's sewing machine and signed up to take a quilting class from a sweet lady named Miss May. I also signed up my sister and my friend, because if it turned out to be a disaster, I figured I'd need moral support.

I went to the quilt shop the week before the class to choose fabrics. I had no idea where to begin, but I was planning to make a quilt for my older daughter, so I brought both girls, ages five and three. I might have been nervous about which fabrics to choose, but my children had no such hang-ups. With their input and some help from Miss May, I left that day with two very excited little girls and enough fabric for two quilts.

I went to the class with my sister, my friend, my borrowed sewing machine, and my fabric. I thought it would be a little stressful, but it was relaxing. I thought I wouldn't be very good at it, but it turns out, I was. I thought I might not really enjoy it, but I loved every minute of it. To this day, that quilting class is one of my favorite memories. I remember being so amazed at how easy it was to create something beautiful. I remember thinking, with every stitch, "I'm going to finish this quilt, and one day my daughter will understand that I made this for her with my own hands, and that I thought of her the entire time." There is love in every fiber of that quilt, and in every quilt I've made since.

I didn't finish that first quilt right away. I got to a certain point in the process and felt uncertain about how to proceed, so I just quit for a little while. One day, my grandmother (whose sewing machine was still sitting on my dining table) said, "You and your sister pick a day and bring those quilts to my house. We're going to finish them." I think she wanted her sewing machine back. At any rate, when my Mammaw gives an order like that, you obey it, so one day, my mom, sister, and I met at her house for lunch and sewing. With their help, I made it through the hard part, and the quilt came together quickly after that. So did the second one, and the third one, etc. Suffice it to say, I bought my own sewing machine.

It's funny that a moment of freaking out about turning thirty started me onto the path of something that would become a lifelong passion. Actually, if the volume of my fabric stash is any indication, it's probably veering more toward an obsession. But making something beautiful for someone is my favorite way to show love, or to celebrate, or to help. And I look back on the process of getting started and realize what making quilts brings to me: time with family and friends, precious moments with my girls, the ability to create something that is uniquely mine and still made especially for someone else. Those first two quilts are on my daughters' beds, keeping them warm every night. And when I tuck them in, they sigh and say, "Wrapped in love!"

It Started With a Quilt

by **JENNY PETTINGER**
Normal, Illinois

Twenty years ago my family and I were living in Tokyo, Japan as a result of a job transfer for my husband's employment. It was the opportunity of a lifetime for our family to experience a different culture. It was obvious we were non-natives simply by the way we looked, and everyone around us kept to themselves and didn't approach us. The vast language barrier also got in the way of connecting with the lovely Japanese people whose country we now called home.

One afternoon I was in the orthodontist's office as my twelve year-old son endured his two hour appointment. To pass the time while waiting in that busy office, I was sewing the binding on a quilt. Suddenly a Japanese mother whose son was also a patient came over and sat down next to me. She then started to admire my quilt and in her limited English started to speak with me. This had never happened to me before, and I was delighted that she felt comfortable in doing this!

Photo Courtesy Jenny Pettinger

I pulled out my English/Japanese dictionary and we communicated with each other by passing the dictionary back and forth. She told me her name was Keiko. A few minutes later the most marvelous thing happened. Keiko invited me to her home. I couldn't believe my ears.

That began a two-year friendship between Keiko, her friend Emiko, and me. Once a month we got together at each other's homes. I taught them how to quilt. They taught me Japanese shodo painting. They taught me how to make sushi. I taught them how to bake my grandma's cinnamon rolls. They taught me a little Japanese. I taught them a little English. It was a wonderful exchange of cultures, and it all started with that quilt.

The Things You Can Find in a Quilt Shop

by **PAMELA & KEN BAGWELL**
Shelbyville, Tennessee

Whenever my husband and I go on vacation, he always indulges me by stopping along the route for me to check out any quilt shops. This particular day he had spotted a billboard advertising a quilt shop, so he dropped me off to shop while he went to find a gas station. After going up and down the aisles admiring the beautiful fabric, I was halfway back to the front of the store when I heard the cashier say, "May I help you, sir?" I glanced up to see that my husband had just walked through the door and heard him say, "Yes, I'm looking for a woman!"

There were about a dozen women in the shop and every head popped up simultaneously looking at the man who just walked in! Immediately I heard him say, "Let me rephrase that. I'm looking for MY woman!" As I got to him everyone was laughing, and a woman stepped from the group and said "Well, I was going to say that I'm high maintenance, but I'm available!" I took him by the arm and said "Honey, let me get you out of here before you get yourself into trouble!" I left with my red-faced husband in tow, and at least one disappointed woman in the quilt shop! We still laugh over this story but have to agree that if you want to find a woman - go to a quilt shop!!

Warming Lives

by **ANITA K. IDLEMAN**
Carthage, Missouri

In the past few years I was privileged to work in our town's rural hospital in the labor and delivery department. We delivered about thirty babies per month. Our community was exceptionally supportive of our birthing center, and the local quilting group lovingly handmade a quilt for every baby born. It was the highlight of our day as nurses to present the new families with one of these beautiful quilts.

Alas, hard economic times and changes in healthcare came to our town, and the decision was made to merge our little hospital with a larger one in the area. Sadly, our birthing center was scheduled to close at the end of the year. The close-knit group of nurses, scrub techs, support staff and administrative leaders mourned the closing, along with the rest of the community.

In memory of the years we had shared, all the employees contributed their old scrubs, and the ladies of the quilting group made a memory

Photo Courtesy Anita K. Idleman

quilt which we presented to our manager at the closing "party" (we called it a wake!) The memory of the years of serving the families of our community live on in that quilt.

And the ladies of the quilting group? They continue to make the baby quilts, and we continue to present them to the new mamas when they come for their postpartum checkup in our local women's clinic. These quilts, hand-stitched with love, continue to warm lives in our small town.

Quilting to Quit

by **CHRISTINA PERRONE**
East Norrition, Pennsylvania

Quilting saved my life, literally. I was a smoker for around thirty years. When I was quilting I would frequently have to wash my hands and material because of that awful smell. When my friend and I got together to quilt I found that I was having so much fun that I really didn't stop to smoke. My friend was a non-smoker, so it wasn't like we took a break to smoke. I finally realized: "What are you doing except making cigarette companies rich and killing yourself?"

I decided that was it. I said to myself I could either buy a pack of cigarettes or a spool of thread and pretty fabric. Well the spool of thread and fabric won and in the meantime so did I. I had tried many times but didn't succeed. I was so happy that it worked. I promised myself that I would invest in my own and others' happiness.

Photo Courtesy Christine Perrone

I'm on the left, Debra Weckenman is in the middle, and Anna Fornace is on the right. If it weren't for these wonderful, beautiful friends of mine I wouldn't be where I am today. They are also my teachers; I have learned so much from them and they are truly angels in disguise.

My heart sings with happiness and joy when I give these quilts away. I know that I'm a stronger person because of all the support of my fellow quilt sisters. It's been six years now since I've quit smoking and I'm expecting my first grandchild sometime in the fall. So here's to quilting for saving my life. This grandma-to-be is so excited, I can't wait to make my grand baby's first quilt!

Preserving Memories

by **DONNA BURR**
Omaha, Nebraska

Whenever I think of my grandma, I think of quilts. She did not speak English, just German, but somehow I understood her. I had an aunt that lived with grandma, my Aunt Millie. She had no control over her muscles, and, oh, I loved her with all my heart. Whenever we went to visit the farm from the big city and visa versa, grandma would bring Aunt Millie. We were inseparable. We always had some type of needlework going. She was the teacher and I was a most attentive student. This relationship went on until she passed away when I was in my late twenties.

Grandma had noticed how I took time to be with my Aunt Millie and it touched her, so she made me a quilt; I was the only grandchild to get one from her. Grandma had twelve children and a ton of grandkids, so the fact that I received this quilt was a great honor.

Years later, I was married and both of these special ladies had passed away, but I had my beautiful quilt. Then one day our house flooded. The creek just couldn't hold all the water. I picked up everything I could before all would be lost. We only got about six inches of water, but the humidity in the house was terrible. My husband came home from work one night to find me sitting on the kitchen with my grandmother's quilt on my lap crying. I was going to save it no matter what. The moisture from the flood got the cotton batting they used so many years ago, and I could only salvage the top of the quilt.

I sat and took out every one of the stitches she had put into the lavender, yellow, and white fabric. I even saw some of the little pinpricks of blood she had left behind. My husband sat down with me and helped me very carefully take this very special piece apart. My two beautiful ladies will always be in my heart and the quilt top in a very special place as well.

It Was Mom's Idea

by **KATHLEEN ROSS**
Ridgecrest, California

A friend of mine was having a baby and before my mom passed she suggested I make her a quilt. I was a garment sewer and knew nothing about quilt making. I looked on the Internet and found videos by Jenny Doan for the Missouri Quilt Co. and I thought maybe I could make a quilt. Then Mom took a turn for the worst and I gave up the idea of the quilt.

I had been my mom's only caregiver for over ten years. Therefore, when she passed away I was lost. My entire life had revolved around taking care of my mother. I literally had to learn to sleep all night and do things for myself. I was sad and lost.

My grieving seemed to last forever. I had promised mom that I would turn her room into my sewing/craft room in the event of her death. My husband knew my mom's wishes and he turned Mom's room into a beautiful sewing room. My husband even bought me a new sewing

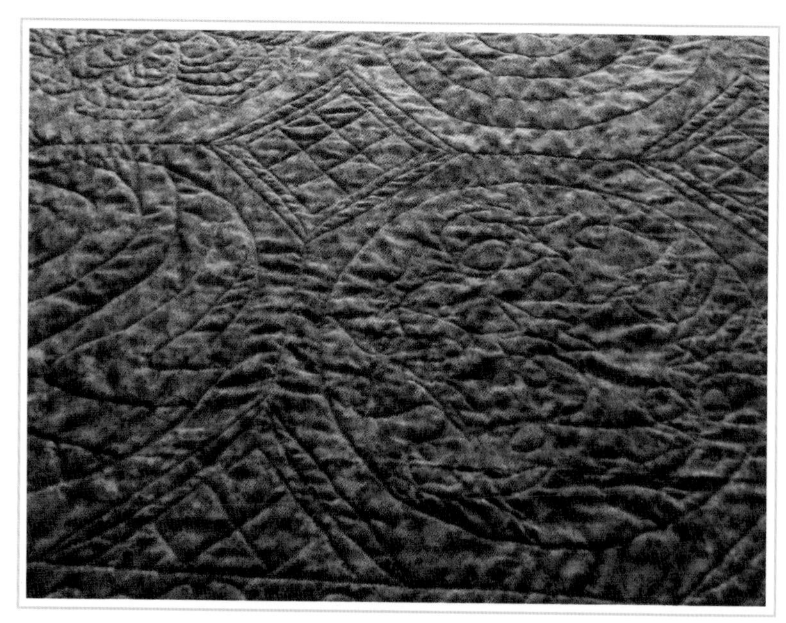

Photo Courtesy Kathleen Ross

machine. I, on the other hand, couldn't bring myself to open the door to Mom's room.

Then I was told my friend was having a girl and her name, although spelled differently, was the same as my mom's: Eleanor. I took this as a sign from Mom to move on and live again. I remembered my mom asking me to make my friend a quilt for her baby.

I went back to those videos, and I constructed my first quilt. I worked through lots of emotions, but this small baby quilt, with all its mistakes, gave me the start of living again.

My mom has been gone for over two years now, and although I still miss her, quilting has given me a life. I truly have found a passion I didn't know I had.

My Mistake

by **DIANA GRANT**
Concord, California

Over the years, I've made lots of mistakes. Seams not straight, quilting with puckers, blocks cut just a little too big or short. Of course I would like to be perfect but the object is to keep someone warm. Besides, God taught me humility years ago.

My Aunt Mary Ellen made quilts for my first two children. She paid for my first quilting class twenty-six years ago while I was pregnant with child number two, an Eleanor Burns Log Cabin class. And when I was pregnant with number three, she said I could make her baby quilt (Mary Ellen's health was declining and I had made several quilts by then.) My quilt guild had been making Sunbonnet Sue and Overall Sam charity quilts, so I decided that would be the quilt I'd make for my baby, Elizabeth.

Somewhere along the way, I'd heard that the Amish always include a mistake in their quilts because only God is perfect. Thinking to myself, "I could be just as humble as the Amish," I decided to put one of my little Sues backwards. I was using an off-white on off-white muslin print. I carefully ironed my backwards facing Sue into place and embroidered her with great care. She was placed in the middle of the third row. I machine quilted Elizabeth's Sunbonnet Sue outlining each of the Sues and finishing with a stitch in the ditch. I was very careful and did a great job.

However, upon closer inspection in the light of day, I saw that I had placed my backwards Sue on the wrong side of the muslin background. It was only noticeably different as part of the whole.

I laughed my head off, God's joke was even better than mine.

Our Civil War Quilt

by **GLADYS I. KITE**
Stockton, California

One of my favorite memories of childhood was when my maternal grandmother came to California from Kansas to spend the winter. She brought a quilt top with her every year. My father built her a quilting frame, and our life revolved around a quilt that took up most of the space in our living room every winter. One of the quilts she made was for my twin bed and it has recently been passed down through my family to my great grandniece. Another covers the bed in my guest room now.

Knowing my love of the quilts she made, when she passed away, Grandma left me a family heirloom quilt made during the American Civil War. My mother shared with me the story behind it.

My great-great grandparents, James and Caroline Gerlach Boston, lived in Illinois. At the outbreak of the war, James enlisted in the Union Army

Photo Courtesy Gladys I. Kite

and went off to fight. When Caroline was notified that James had been wounded and had been taken to Benton Barracks, Missouri, she left her children with her mother and went to care for him.

She stayed for the duration of the war, caring for her husband and many other wounded soldiers. During this time, she made a spool pattern quilt and, in each of the four trapezoids of every block, she embroidered the name, home state, and unit of each soldier she cared for. Near the center of the quilt is a block with her name, and across from it, her husband's.

For a quilt 150 years old, it is in remarkable condition. It reminds me of the long line of women who preceded me for whom needlework in all its forms is a joy!

The Sister Quilt

by **BECKY BENOIT**
Chestermere, Alberta

Six years ago on a blustery March day, my nephew was born. As his tiny body slipped into the world and into the waiting hands of a neonatal intensive-care team, the lives of our entire family changed in an instant.

My sister Erin and I have always been best friends. Born four years earlier, I've always felt a motherly sense of protection for my little sister, and even as we argued over toys as children, or scrapped over borrowed clothing and makeup as teens, our bond has remained rock-solid. When Erin woke, terrified by the boogeyman in the darkest hours of the night, it was always my room she fled to, crawling under the covers and snuggling up to me for comfort. And when I needed an ear to listen or a shoulder to cry on, I always turned to my resilient, plucky younger sister for support.

When Erin and her husband welcomed their first child, little Graham David Burr, into the world six weeks early, we had no idea of the long journey that awaited our family. Erin's pregnancy was normal, so when Graham was born with a multitude of health issues, it came as a shock to all of us. Diagnosed with a rare genetic disorder called CHARGE Syndrome, Graham was born with hearing and visual impairment, facial palsy, kidney and heart problems, breathing issues, and trouble swallowing. In the first tenuous days of his life, his very survival hung in the balance when doctors detected a serious brain hemorrhage. In the weeks that followed, the tiny ginger-haired baby underwent a series of surgeries, including heart surgery, insertion of a feeding tube, and a tracheotomy to help him breathe. Little Graham didn't even come home from the hospital until he was four months old.

During that time, my sister and I clung to each other for support. After the shock of hearing Graham's diagnosis for the first time, I remember curling up under the covers in my sister's bed once again, just as we had as kids, as I tried to comfort her and reassure her that everything would be okay.

As weeks and then months went by, my sister discovered a new kind of normal. Instead of play-dates and baby food, my sister's days were spent visiting specialists and learning how to use a suction machine and a feeding pump. But while there were many challenges, there were so many small victories too, moments of triumph that lifted her spirits and kept her going when things got difficult.

When Graham smiled at his mother's voice for the first time a few days after getting a cochlear implant which finally allowed him to hear, it was a huge moment for all of us. The usual milestones take on so much more significance when you think about how hard Graham has had to work to accomplish them.

Up until this time, quilting was just one of many hobbies I liked to do when I could find a few spare minutes. I'd never tackled anything really complex, always sticking to fairly basic patterns and techniques and familiar color palettes. But as I watched my sister grow and change, becoming a truly inspiring mother and a fierce advocate for her own child and others with special needs, I was inspired to make her something special, a quilt that matched her plucky personality and would provide the warmth and comfort she needed when I couldn't be there for her in person.

With this mission, I embarked on a quilting journey of my own. Armed with a few dog-eared books from my quilting library, I set out to learn how to paper piece, and then headed off to my favorite local quilt store in search of a rainbow of 1930s reproduction fabrics. Not only did I need to learn how to paper piece, I was also determined to quilt the finished project myself on my own machine, so I had another steep learning curve to surmount as I learned how to pin-baste, stitch-in-the-ditch, free-motion quilt, and mark patterns.

Photos Courtesy Becky Benoit

Finally, after many, many hours of hard work, my masterpiece was completed. I still remember the moment I handed the quilt to my sister, and how the bright white background fabric darkened to gray in the places where her grateful tears splashed it.

Today, my quilt occupies a place of honor in the Burr household. While my sister loves to cuddle under it with a warm cup of tea and a good book, she's got competition. Graham has adopted the quilt as his own, choosing it as his favorite place to curl up for a nap when he's tired. And when Graham's not cuddled up in it, if I look closely, I can almost see two little girls curled up in its warm depths, whispering secrets in the dark and dreaming about what the future will hold.